Wolves

and Other Wild Dogs

Concept and Product Development: Editorial Options, Inc.
Series Designer: Karen Donica
Book Author: Mary E. Reid

**For information on other World Book
products, visit us at our Web site at
http://www.worldbook.com**

**For information on sales to schools and
libraries in the United States, call 1-800-975-3250.**

**For information on sales to schools and
libraries in Canada, call 1-800-837-5365.**

World Book, Inc.
233 N. Michigan Ave.
Chicago, Il 60601

Library of Congress Cataloging-in-Publication Data

Reid, Mary E.
     Wolves and other wild dogs / [book author, Mary E. Reid].
         p. cm.—(World Book's animals of the world)
     Summary: Questions and answers explore the world of wild dogs, with an emphasis on wolves.
     ISBN 0-7166-1206-2 -- ISBN 0-7166-1200-3 (set)
     1. Wolves—Juvenile literature. 2. Canidae—Juvenile literature. [I. Wolves—Miscellanea. 2. Wild
dogs—Miscellanea. 3. Canidae—Miscellanea. 4. Questions and answers.] I. World Book, Inc. II. Title.
III. Series.

QL737.C22 R44 2000
599.773—dc21   00-021636

Printed in Singapore

1 2 3 4 5 6 7 8 9 05 04 03 02 01 00

World Book's Animals of the World

Wolves
and Other Wild Dogs

How can I make a long distance call?

World Book, Inc.
A Scott Fetzer Company
Chicago

Contents

Who wants to play fetch?

Who leaps for lunch?

Who keeps his cool?

What Is a Wild Dog?

Wolves, pet dogs, and their relatives all belong to the dog family. They are also called canids, from *canis,* the Latin word for *dog.* Wild dogs do not live with humans as pet dogs do. Foxes, coyotes, and jackals are also wild dogs.

Wild dogs are carnivores *(KAHR nuh vawrz),* or meat eaters. They have four long fangs called canines, or dog teeth. These teeth help wild dogs hold onto struggling prey.

Wolves and most other wild dogs have long legs for their body size. These help the dogs run swiftly and make them stand tall, so that they can see far across the land. Long, bushy tails help the animals keep their balance and make fast turns as they run. Wild dogs can dig and swim, too.

Wolves and their relatives have excellent eyesight. They also have a powerful sense of smell. And their ears can hear a far greater range of sounds than human ears can.

Gray wolf

Where in the World Do Wolves Live?

Wolves once hunted all over North America, Europe, and Asia. They occupied a larger territory than any other land mammal, except humans. Wolves lived in every kind of habitat, from forests to plains, and from mountains to swamps. On the map, you can see where wolves used to live and where they live now.

Today, wolves are almost extinct in many of their natural habitats. Many wolves disappeared because people hunted and killed them. Others gradually vanished as the great forests and grasslands were made into farms, highways, and cities.

World Map

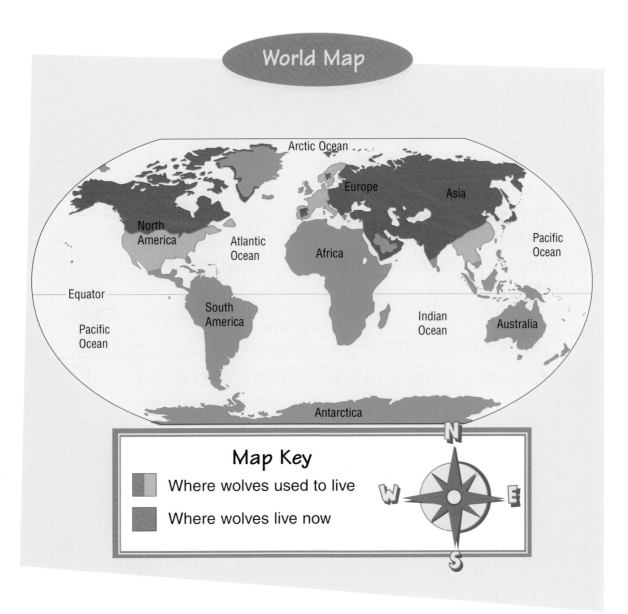

Arctic Ocean

Europe

Asia

North America

Atlantic Ocean

Africa

Pacific Ocean

Equator

Pacific Ocean

South America

Indian Ocean

Australia

Antarctica

Map Key

Where wolves used to live

Where wolves live now

N

W   E

S

How Are Wolves Like Pet Dogs?

Scientists think that pet dogs descended from wolves thousands of years ago. The bodies of wolves and pet dogs are still much alike in shape, although wolves are larger and heavier than most dogs. A male adult wolf is about 2 1/2 feet (76 centimeters) tall at the shoulder. A male weighs about 75 to 120 pounds (34 to 54 kilograms). Female wolves are slightly smaller than males.

All members of the dog family, including wolves, run on the fronts of their paws. Most members have five toes on each front paw and four on each back paw. One of the front toes, the dewclaw, does not touch the ground. It is located on the back of the paw.

Wolves and pet dogs are both social animals and good communicators. Most pet dogs are friendly to each other and to humans. Wolves are friendly toward other pack members. But just as most pet dogs guard their homes, wolves protect their territory. Like pet dogs, wolves have a playful side, too.

Gray wolf pup

Why Do Wolves Live in Packs?

Wolves don't have easy lives. Often they have to travel many miles to find prey. And most wolves don't catch every animal they hunt. Their prey have strong defenses. Deer and caribou can run faster than wolves. Huge musk oxen fight off wolves by standing in a circle with their horns facing out.

To help them catch prey, wolves live and hunt in packs of 8 to 12 members. Each pack stakes out a large territory as its hunting ground. Wolves mark the territory by urinating along its border. They fiercely defend the territory against other wolf packs. The territory is important because it's where adult wolves find food for themselves and their young.

Large packs of wolves can more easily capture large prey. For example, a large pack might attack a moose rather than a deer. Pack hunting is especially important when pups are born. A litter of pups may need more meat than two parents alone can provide.

Timber wolf pack
in meadow

Who Is the Leader of the Pack?

Each pack has a dominant male wolf that is the leader. This wolf is called the alpha male. The alpha male helps keep order among the pack members. He also leads the hunt. Being in charge has its rewards, too. The dominant wolves always eat first after a kill.

Other pack members often include the alpha male's mate (called the alpha female), their pups, and the alpha male's brothers and sisters.

When pack members meet the leader, they use body language to show their respect. They crouch down with their ears flattened and tails low. This is their way of saying, "You are the leader."

Members of a wolf pack also have a greeting ceremony. This takes place just before or after a hunt. The wolves wag tails and lick one another's faces. They rush to the leader and show their loyalty by sticking their muzzles in his face.

Alpha male with pack

What Makes Wolves Good Hunters?

Wolves have several features that help them hunt prey. Wolves have excellent hearing. They also have a keen sense of smell. Wolves can smell a deer from over 1 mile (1.6 kilometers) away!

Wolves have very good eyesight, too. A wolf's eyes are in the front of its head. A wolf can see its prey with both eyes at once. Its vision in the dark is very good, and it can easily spot movement.

Wolves have long legs that help them run fast. A wolf can run for 12 miles at 15 to 30 miles (24 to 48 kilometers) per hour. Over a short distance, it can sprint as fast as 40 miles (64 kilometers) per hour.

Wolves use their sharp canine teeth to hold onto prey. Wolves have very strong jaws that can crunch the huge bones of moose and other large prey.

Gray wolf hunting rabbit

How Do Wolves Hunt?

Wolves usually hunt in a pack. This makes them more efficient hunters. Each hunt may take several hours. As the wolves set out, they often run in a single line to search for prey.

The wolves may find a herd of caribou or musk oxen. The pack will usually choose a weak or old animal as its prey. Such an animal is almost always easier to catch than a young, healthy one. The wolves then sneak toward the animal. They stay downwind so that the prey cannot smell them. Once they are close, the wolves start to run. They attack the animal's rump or sides. As the animal weakens and stumbles, the wolves grab it by the throat or snout. Then they quickly kill it.

Pack members work well together. Some wolves may distract a mother animal while the others sneak up on her young. Or a few wolves may go ahead of the pack and hide. They ambush the prey when the rest of the pack drives it toward them.

Arctic wolf pack
with musk oxen

Why Do Wolves Howl?

Wolves howl for many reasons. Sometimes, wolves howl to claim their territory. Their howls warn other wolves to stay away. On a calm night, their howling can be heard from up to 10 miles (16 kilometers) away. Sometimes one pack howls, saying "This is our territory." Other packs howl back, saying "This is ours."

Howling helps pack members keep in touch when they get separated. It also helps them get together again. No two wolves have exactly the same voice. When they are separated, wolves probably recognize one another's howls, just as we recognize the voices of our friends on the telephone.

Wolves also howl just because they like to! Some people think the howls of wolves sound a lot like a group sing-along. Howling together helps keep up a strong group feeling in a pack.

Gray wolf howling

How Else Do Wolves Signal Each Other?

Wolves have many ways to communicate with one another. One way is with sounds. In addition to howling, wolves use a variety of other sounds to "talk" to each other. An alpha wolf may growl at another wolf. The other wolf may whine or squeal.

Wolves also use body language. For example, a wolf may crouch down before the pack leader. Or a wolf may signal "Let's play!" with forelegs down, rump up, and tail wagging—just as a pet dog does.

Wolves also use their tails to communicate their status in the pack. A wolf may curl its tail under its body when it is with the alpha wolf.

Wolves sometimes show feelings with their faces. They make threatening or "Don't hurt me" expressions. Good communications among pack members helps keep order and enables the pack to work together successfully.

"Talking" wolves

What Are Newborn Wolf Pups Like?

Usually only the alpha male and female in a wolf pack breed. They mate in winter. Then the female prepares a den. She may take over an old fox's den. Or she may dig a new den in a sandy hillside near a stream or lake. The tunnel leading into the den may be 15 feet (4.5 meters) long.

After two months, the female gives birth to a litter of from 1 to 11 pups. A newborn wolf pup is blind, deaf, and helpless. It needs its mother's warmth to keep a steady body temperature. The pups spend their first days living in the den and drinking their mother's milk.

After three weeks, the pups begin to explore outside and to eat meat. They beg for meat by licking the lips of their mother or another adult wolf. The adult coughs up some of the meat it has recently eaten, and the pups eat it.

Gray wolf and pups

What Is a Pup-Sitter?

A pup-sitter watches over the pups while the mother goes hunting. The pup-sitter is usually a "lower-class" member of the pack. The sitter may be a brother or a sister from the previous year's litter. Or the sitter may be an inexperienced hunter.

Through the summer, the den is a center of activity for the pack. The adults go off to hunt in the evening, as a pack or in small groups. When the hunters come back in the morning, the pups mob them and beg for food. The pup-sitter may also beg for food. Sometimes, pup-sitting can be very tiring!

When they are 2 months old, the pups no longer need the den. The pack relocates to an open-air home called a rendezvous *(RAHN deh voo)* site, or meeting place.

Gray wolf pup-sitter

What Games Do Wolf Pups Play?

Wolf pups chase, wrestle, and pounce on one another. They play with objects they find, too. As they win or lose at play fights, they work out a dominance order among themselves. The winners of play fights make it clear that they are more powerful than the losers are. Winning at play shows that they can dominate their less powerful brothers and sisters.

Playing also helps pups develop their muscles and practice the skills they will need for hunting. They sneak up and pounce on insects and small animals. At first, the pups often miss. But they are quick learners!

In the fall, the pups and adults begin to hunt together. The pups learn by watching the older wolves. It takes time and practice for a young wolf to become a skilled hunter.

Wolf pups playing

How Do Wolves Survive in the Arctic?

The wolf you see here is an Arctic wolf. Notice how its white fur blends with the snowy background. This makes it difficult for the wolf's prey to see it coming.

The fur of an Arctic wolf is very thick. It needs to be! In winter, temperatures in the Arctic can drop to –70 °F (–57 °C). To stay warm, Arctic wolves grow an extra layer of fur in winter. This makes their legs look very thick. At night, the wolf curls up with its legs close to its warm body. It wraps its fluffy tail over its face.

Arctic wolves are not born white. Pups are usually born after the snow melts. Newborn pups are a gray-brown color. This helps camouflage *(KAM uh flahzh),* or hide, them during their first summer. It's a good thing, too, because some birds of prey and other animals kill and eat these pups.

Arctic Wolf

Do Wolves Ever Live Alone?

Sometimes, wolves do leave their packs. A wolf may leave because it has been mistreated by other members. An alpha wolf might go off on its own if it has been replaced by a new alpha wolf.

Living alone can be very dangerous for a wolf. A lone wolf must be careful if it wanders into the territories of wolf packs. Wolf packs may chase the lone wolf off. The packs may even fight the lone wolf and kill it. A lone wolf must also find and kill enough food by itself. This is often very difficult.

If everything goes well, a lone wolf will eventually find a mate. Together, the two may even form a pack and establish a territory of their own.

Lone wolf

Do Other Wild Dogs Compete with Wolves?

Yes, coyotes do! And coyotes have been more successful than wolves. The reason is that coyotes adapt better than wolves. Unlike wolves, coyotes can live almost anywhere. They thrive in grasslands, but they can also live well in forests, on mountains, and in arctic regions.

Coyotes used to live mainly on the plains of western North America. But they expanded into forests as their biggest rival, the wolf, disappeared from those areas. With no wolves to compete with, coyotes grew and grew in number. Today, coyotes are found all the way from Alaska to Central America.

Another reason coyotes are so successful is that they eat almost anything! Their prey include rabbits, gophers, mice, squirrels, prairie dogs, reptiles, and insects. Coyotes also eat carrion, or the remains of dead animals. Coyotes eat fruit and seeds, too. They even have a soft spot for watermelon!

Coyote

How Do Coyotes Hunt?

Unlike wolves, most coyotes live alone or in pairs. But they sometimes do form packs to hunt. In a pack, coyotes can attack large prey, such as antelope and deer. A pack of coyotes may have from three to eight members. After the hunt, pack members often go their separate ways.

Coyotes are extremely fast runners. In fact, they are among the fastest mammals in North America. Not many animals can outrun a coyote.

Coyotes are also clever. Sometimes they hunt alongside badgers. Badgers are fierce little animals. They are also very good diggers. A badger may watch as a coyote chases a rabbit into a hole. Then the badger digs into the hole and catches the rabbit. Both the badger and the coyote share the kill.

Coyote and badger

How Do Foxes Fit In?

Foxes look like small, slim dogs. They have bushy tails, large ears, and pointed snouts. The fox doesn't need a wolf's large, heavy jaw. Its prey is much smaller than a wolf's prey.

Foxes hunt alone and at night. They have keen hearing and an excellent sense of smell. A fox can locate a mouse to eat just by listening to its squeaks in the grass.

Foxes live and hunt in a territory that they mark with their scent. They defend it against intruders. Like coyotes, foxes eat whatever they can catch— mice, ground squirrels, rabbits, birds, frogs, lizards, and insects. Foxes also seem to like fruit, even when other food is available.

Red fox

Which Wild Dogs Are Most Like Cats?

Red foxes are a lot like cats in the way they hunt. The fox you see here is a red fox. It is doing a "mousing leap." A red fox may sneak up on its prey, freeze, and then leap and pounce. Its prey is often a mouse.

Like cats, red foxes have whiskers that help them feel their way in the dark and sense what is around them. Red foxes can see in the dark, too, so they are good night hunters. The pupils of their eyes are vertical slits, just like a cat's eyes. The pupils open very wide to gather light. A fox's eyes also have special layers that help collect light.

Red fox

Which Wild Dogs Climb Trees?

If something is chasing a gray fox, the fox may run for a hole. Or it may climb a tree! The gray fox grasps the tree trunk with its front paws and pushes up with its hind feet. It may even leap from branch to branch.

Gray foxes don't just climb trees. They may even make their dens in tree hollows. These hollows can be as high as 30 feet (9 meters) off the ground!

Gray foxes have a very large habitat. It extends from the border between the United States and Canada in North America all the way to Venezuela and Colombia in South America. Gray foxes hunt in woodlands and on open plains. They also live near the edges of cities and on farmlands.

Gray foxes eat insects, birds, and small mammals, such as rabbits and mice. Gray foxes also eat plant foods, such as fruits and grains.

Gray fox

Just How Swift Are Swift Foxes?

Swift foxes are some of the fastest wild dogs in North America. They can run more than 25 miles (40 kilometers) an hour over short distances. Swift foxes are also known as kit foxes because they are about the same size as kittens. They are usually no more than 20 inches (51 centimeters) long and weigh from 4 to 6 pounds (1.8 to 2.7 kilograms).

With great bursts of speed, swift foxes can chase down almost any mouse, ground squirrel, cricket, or other small prey. Swift foxes also use their incredible quickness to zigzag their way to safety when chased by coyotes, red foxes, or other predators.

Swift fox

How Do Bat-Eared Foxes Keep Cool?

The ears are a clue! Bat-eared foxes are little animals with very big ears. They live in dry areas of eastern and southern Africa. Like other animals that live in hot regions, the bat-eared fox needs to keep itself cool. This fox's ears allow heat from its body to pass into the air.

How big are the ears of this little fox? The fox itself is only 18 to 23 inches (46 to 58 centimeters) high at the shoulder. But its ears are up to 5 inches (13 centimeters) long!

Bat-eared foxes eat mainly insects, especially termites. They also like fruits, mice, and rats. This fox has more teeth than any other wild dog. With 46 to 50 teeth, the bat-eared fox is able to chew through the hard parts of an insect's body.

Bat-eared fox

Which Foxes Are the Smallest?

The smallest of all foxes are fennecs. A fennec is about 16 inches (41 centimeters) long and weighs only 2 to 3 pounds (0.9 kilogram to 1.4 kilograms). Fennecs live in the deserts of Saudi Arabia and northern Africa.

A fennec is well suited to the hot climate in which it lives. Body heat escapes easily through the fennec's huge ears. Hairs on the pads of its feet allow it to run quickly over loose or hot sand. To get moisture in its diet, a fennec eats the roots of desert plants that it digs up.

Fennecs can use their enormous ears to pick up sounds made by their prey. They usually hunt small animals, such as gerbils, lizards, and insects. But sometimes they kill rabbits bigger than themselves!

Fennecs

What Are Dingoes?

Dingoes are wild dogs of Australia. They usually live alone or in small family groups. Dingoes are very shy animals. They seldom allow themselves to be seen. They can survive in all kinds of habitats—including deserts and rain forests.

Dingoes eat whatever is available, but they favor rabbits and wallabies. They also hunt rodents and lizards. When going after large prey, such as kangaroos, dingoes sometimes hunt in a pack.

Many Europeans who settled in Australia in the late 1700's raised sheep. Dingoes already lived in the area. They killed the sheep. Ever since then, the dingoes themselves have been hunted and killed.

Dingo

Which Wild Dogs Whistle While They Work?

Dholes *(DOHLZ)* hunt in packs of 5 to 20 members. They are also called whistling hunters. When dholes hunt, they make howling whistles. Whistling helps the dholes keep in touch and work together to make the kill.

Dholes live in Asia. They have widely different habitats. Their homeland extends from the mountains of the Himalayas *(HIH muh LAY uhz)* to the tropical forests of Malaysia *(muh LAY zhuh)*.

What dholes eat depends on where they live. In Siberia, they hunt reindeer. In the mountains of Tibet, they kill wild sheep. In India, they often prey on deer.

Dholes gang up on their prey and run it down. A pack of dholes sometimes drives a leopard or a tiger away from its own kill.

Dhole pack

Which Wild Dogs Are Street Cleaners?

Golden jackals clean up villages and towns of northern Africa, southern Asia, and southeastern Europe. These animals eat garbage and carrion. Left alone, the garbage and meat would rot. This might attract rats and other pests, causing disease. Thankfully, golden jackals make meals out of many of these messes.

Golden jackals are definitely not picky eaters. They hunt almost any small animal, including hares and rodents, such as rats. Since rodents damage crops, the jackals help farmers.

Golden jackal

Which Wild Dogs Share and Share Alike?

Though fierce hunters, African hunting dogs have a nice side, too. Hunting dogs let pups eat first after a kill. If the pups are very young, adults will eat meat and then cough it up for the pups. Adults also do this for sick and weak dogs.

African hunting dogs are also called African wild dogs. And they are wild looking! They are covered from head to toe with black, white, and brownish-yellow blotches. Each of these animals has its own unique pattern.

These wild dogs are very good hunters. They may kill as many as 9 out of 10 animals they hunt. Their strategy is to outrun their prey, knock it down, and then tear its body open.

African hunting dogs

57

Which Wild Dogs Don't Look Like Dogs?

Raccoon dogs have black masks, just as raccoons do. And their mouths do not look like the mouths of other wild dogs. Raccoon dogs usually have smaller teeth. Their molars, or back teeth, are larger and are used for grinding the plants they eat.

Raccoon dogs live in Asia. They eat plants, fish, frogs, and insects. In the colder parts of Asia, some raccoon dogs fatten up in the fall and hibernate in a burrow through the winter.

Bush dogs are rare animals that look more like miniature bears than dogs. They have small ears, short legs, and short tails. They live in Central and South America.

Bush dogs live in groups and spend a lot of time in the water. They hunt pacas *(PAH kuhz)* and capybaras *(KAP uh BAHR uhz)*, which are large rodents.

Raccoon dog

Are Wild Dogs in Danger?

Some dogs are in danger. Red wolves are nearly extinct. Gray wolves now live in only a small part of the land they once hunted. People and lions have killed great numbers of African wild dogs. These dogs have also lost much of their habitat to farms.

Other wild dogs, such as coyotes and the red foxes, now live in more places than ever before. Their numbers continue to grow and grow.

Many laws have been passed to stop the killing of endangered wolves. Conservationists are working to preserve national parks and forests. They want to give plenty of space to wild dogs and their prey.

In the United States, scientists have been reintroducing wolves in places where they used to live. One such place is Yellowstone National Park. Wolves had lived in the park for many years. Scientists and many others hope that the wolves will, once again thrive there.

Red wolf

Wild Dog Fun Facts

→ Coyotes and domesticated dogs sometimes mate. The offspring are called coydogs.

→ The daring film hero Zorro is named after a wild dog. *Zorro* means *fox* in Spanish.

→ Raccoon dogs growl and whine, but they never bark.

→ Adult bat-eared foxes never wag their tails.

→ A wolf may eat up to 20 pounds (9 kilograms) of meat at one meal.

→ The South American maned wolf has such long legs that it has been called the fox on stilts.

→ Fennecs can go for days without drinking water.

→ A weasellike animal lived 500 million years ago. That animal is the ancestor of today's dog family. It is also the ancestor of cats, bears, raccoons, and weasels.

Glossary

adapt To adjust to new conditions or surroundings.

alpha The first letter of the Greek alphabet. In English, it means the first, or the beginning, of something.

alpha wolf The leader of a wolf pack.

Arctic An ice-covered region surrounding the North Pole.

camouflage To change in appearance in order to hide.

canid A member of the dog family.

canines Four long, pointed dog teeth.

carnivore An animal that eats mostly meat.

carrion Dead or decaying flesh or meat that is not fit to be eaten by people.

den A sheltered area where a wolf mother raises her pups until they are 2 months old.

dewclaw An extra toe on the forelegs of all dogs. Some dogs also have dewclaws on their hind legs.

dominant Most powerful or important.

extinct Died out and never seen again.

pack A group of wild dogs.

predator Any animal that preys on another animal.

prey Any animal that is hunted for food by another animal.

pupil The opening in the center of the iris (colored part) of the eye through which light enters. The pupil gets smaller in bright light and larger in dim light.

rendezvous site An unsheltered area where a wolf pack will relocate after pups are 2 months old.

urinate To pass urine from the body.

65

Index

(**Boldface** indicates a photo, map or illustration.)

Picture Acknowledgements: Front & Back Cover: © Tom & Pat Leeson, Photo Researchers; © Hans Reinhard, Bruce Coleman Inc.; © W. Perry Conway, Tom Stack & Associates; © Stephen J. Krasemann, Bruce Coleman Collection; © Norman Tomalin, Bruce Coleman Collection.

© F. Aberham/IFA from Bruce Coleman Inc. 2, 21; © Erwin & Peggy Bauer, Bruce Coleman Inc. 5, 27, 29, 33, 41, 45; © Wolfgang Bayer, Bruce Coleman Inc. 15, 57; © Tom Brakefield, Bruce Coleman Inc. 13; © Jim Brandenburg, Minden Pictures 19, 25; © W. Perry Conway, Tom Stack & Associates 35; © Gary Kramer 55; © Stephen J. Krasemann, Bruce Coleman Collection 7, 39; © W. Lankinen, Bruce Coleman Inc. 61; © Frans Lanting, Minden Pictures 5, 47; © Jeff Lepore, Photo Researchers 4, 11; © Mark Newman, Bruce Coleman Inc. 49; © Hans Reinhard, Bruce Coleman Inc. 59; © Jeffrey Rich Nature Photography 23; © Mark Stouffer, Animals Animals 37; © Norman Tomalin, Bruce Coleman Collection, 51; © Staffan Widstrand, Bruce Coleman Collection 31; © Rod Williams, Bruce Coleman Inc. 43, 53.

Illustrations: WORLD BOOK illustration by Karen Donica 9; .WORLD BOOK illustration by Patricia Stein 62.